# STASH
# Of
# THE STREET

MARSHAL MUHAGA

First published in Great Britain in 2023 by:
Carnelian Heart Publishing Ltd
Suite A
82 James Carter Road
Mildenhall
Suffolk
IP28 7DE
UK

www.carnelianheartpublishing.co.uk

©Marshal Muhaga 2023

Paperback ISBN    978-1-914287-51-0
eBook ISBN        978-1-914287-52-7

All rights reserved. No part of this publication may be reproduced, stored in a retrieval system or transmitted in any form or by any means, electronic, mechanical, photocopying, recording or otherwise without prior written permission from the publisher.

Editor: Samantha Rumbidzai Vazhure

Cover design:
Artwork - Rukodzi Art
Layout - Rebeca Covers

Interior:
Typeset by Carnelian Heart Publishing Ltd
Layout and formatting by DanTs Media

# Introduction

All mankind being equal and independent, no one ought to harm another's health, life and liberty. It all happened so fast. The hate. The ghetto. The migration. The wars. The fiery altar upon which mankind was meant to be sacrificed.

I can't help but think that over the ages, mankind has tried many ways to combat the forces of evil…prayer, fasting, good works and so on. It appears, up until Doomsday, no one seemed to have thought about gun-powder, war, love, hate, loneliness, racism…

This book is a collection of conversations I had, would have and heard as I grew up.

I was young
when I told myself,

"I cannot go to Verkhoyansk & Oymyakon
where storms fast descend
cold winds burning faces like frosty peppers.

I was South of the Equator
when I fancied pure fluffy snow
like angels on the floor,
children of the North
shouting with glee
as they slid on sledges down a slope
their parents scraping ice with shovels,
building snowmen before clouds gathered again
and kept everyone locked.

yet, I still loved my South

where the Sun sits upon hills
like a great Sombrero hat,
where music & dances flow into one another
like waves…
while Jahmans come together
and light up Sativa."

## Table of Contents

| | |
|---|---:|
| I Love the Street my Father Walked | 2 |
| We Were Homeless in Between | 3 |
| One Day | 4 |
| Whole Again | 5 |
| The One That Left | 7 |
| Isn't It Our Last Separation? | 8 |
| The End of Us | 9 |
| Longing For You Kills Me | 11 |
| Let Me Go | 12 |
| Fool Or Sage? | 13 |
| Hopes Will Bloom One Day | 15 |
| Once Upon a Midnight | 16 |
| Your Favourite Song | 17 |
| We Were Guests | 18 |
| The Valleys Down | 19 |
| Maputi neMabhodhoro | 20 |
| The Noise Maker | 21 |
| The Great MaShona Model | 22 |
| The Night Passed | 23 |
| Survivor | 24 |

| | |
|---|---|
| We Shall Suffer If We Don't Hear | 25 |
| Same Song | 26 |
| Rolling Stone | 27 |
| Boats of No Captains | 28 |
| Pygmy Among Giants | 29 |
| Blank Page | 30 |
| Buried Bridge | 31 |
| The Devil Promised Evil at Full Throttle | 32 |
| Fight or Flee | 33 |
| First Slice of Bread | 34 |
| Addiction | 35 |
| Awful Greed | 36 |
| Migration Was Better Than Home | 37 |
| Gukura… | 39 |
| If I Don't Make It Home | 40 |
| "I Must Arise!" | 41 |
| Letter from The Dead | 42 |
| Harare Hairarwe | 43 |
| Forced to Fuck Ghosts | 45 |
| Click-Clack | 46 |
| Affixed to the Slaughterhouse | 47 |
| Cemetery | 48 |

Pain                                                      49

Lost Diary                                                50

How Two Cities Worship The Rising Sun                     51

Neighbour                                                 52

Like Two Odd Socks                                        53

Our World                                                 54

Stash of The Street                                       55

When the Time Comes                                       57

**Glossary of Shona and Zimbabwean colloquial terminology** 59

For Sperile and Killy, my parents.
And for Khalifa, Shelly, Oncemore and friends who became family.
You're all great.

# I Love the Street my Father Walked

Merely one of the surging crowds
toiling, day after day
along that thin-long street
he used to go out,
and from it he came back home
like waves hitting the river banks.
I like the street my father walked

in dark valleys, difficult seasons…
in projected positivity, and laughter…
it was that street for the umpteenth time

Even when I'm lost
that street appears before my eyes;
the stones he stepped on are there;
His foot prints are there;
His smell is there;

The magic of that street
is the mingling of the errand and the mien
Still, still the shadows stay
with my feet upon the moonlight dust
that lies subdued now, come dew, come rust

## We Were Homeless in Between

Neither our place nor our homeland is known;
We were homeless,
We landed like a migratory bird;
We were homeless in between.

Our wants were few, but we found
Our peace, from the ground & nature.
God's friendly bushes were our 'pad'
They gave us what little ease we had.

They told us that there is yours, this here is ours.
They didn't give us a home to live in;
They stationed us here and there
We were homeless in between.

We lived in slammers of sensitivity;
Feeling far too much, for nothing.
Our migration did not land on plains;
We wandered in streams and hills;
We were homeless in between.

Winding paths and abandoned alley led us nowhere
Sweet songs of nature went unheard
The heart still desired its own homeland
Steppes turned to barren land
We were homeless in between

## One Day

One day you'll look back
like Lot's wife
and regret everything you did
to let it end.

You'll dream about me,
but I'll be dreaming of someone else
and your best dreams
will turn into nightmares
as I shrivel and vanish
while your wanting flares up to a special place
beyond the stars, moon and space,
broken with piercing explosions,
burning afflictions & hollers
of agonising cries
as you turn into a pillar of salt.

You'll be tethered by shadows of yesteryears' love
and you'll wait for an echo
gone comatose,
but I won't be there
like Gomorrah.

## Whole Again

I can't look at the glimmering night sky;
not even at the luminous stars;
my eyes once admired.

You won't find me waiting outside in the dark
for your key to unlock the door
as I did before, with open arms to hold you close,
and keep you warm;
when you didn't take my hand
I suffered in a trainwreck
that was once life,
deluxe thoughts of 'Us'
made me allergic to myself

Perhaps you find comfort
in the heart of another,
I see it engraved on your face
that we've been finished
for a while.

It was a torture of sorts,
to sit alone in a lifeless union
embroiled of secret thoughts,
and you promised to be my love
but failed to be my friend.

I may be half empty,
but in losing you
I have gained

serenity and love.

As I move forward
with a carefree smile,
I will be made whole
again, by time,
as I cross every mile.

## The One That Left

From a lineage of times
traipsing through centuries,
in search of each other
we longed for completion
till we met like fire and cigarettes

We thought the winds
would free us
but liberty demented us
like twin flames taking flight
from backfire.

We cannot undo what is done,
We are restless winds
that morphed into a storm;
and tore through the place it called home.

Heedless of where home is,
we stray about,
yesteryears whisper
washing our faces
birthing the erasure of euphoria
as our Genesis— Unheard
bears no fruit...

## Isn't It Our Last Separation?

If partying bells sound suddenly
will you say goodbye, darling?

If I kneel in front of you to say 'stay'
will you go away
like tidal river bore
hopeless, like helpless beaux?

We were young and happy
and let the world be our oyster,
we're not from here,
all is kismet until death.

If the universe says we're destined for each other
separation will aid our better selves.
Let's wait for our Renaissance
as we learn to embrace our truth,
with ceaseless sighs,
for we crossed these depths
pursuing our love
behind the moon
where dreams grow
but we failed to unite the sky with hills.

## The End of Us

He loved mint liqueur
even if he forgets me.
He was my Italian espresso
with aromatic seduction—
I became addicted.

He might've likened me to something too:
...the wet fragrance of wild flowers
Or honeyed milk...or something bitter

Yes, I wrote our end
when I was headed for dead ends,
he touched me in all the left places
where my soul begged to be felt
yet he failed and ran me into the ground

They are lucky to have him
those who took my place by his side
to help him find
what he failed to find in me.

My heart used to bleed for him
but it dried up
as I coughed up the shit
of him each morning,
mouthful of bile
till I traded wisdom
for freedom
to fill the void

that yawned within me,
without him.

## Longing For You Kills Me

Should death beckon me
and whisper of an unknown land
you'll never see me again,
roads that forge links between us are tied
and what binds us is trust
ah, bitter is the trial to live in different worlds
like stray beasts

It doesn't feel like home anymore,
these miles make us two sets of footprints
or divergent birds
when we're meant to be intertwined
like main branches on a family tree

I long to be with you,
I search for you through cities,
with renewed vigour I search again
hoping to see you
yet I know between us is a distance
that is Aphelion

This craving makes me a prisoner
waiting for freedom
like Mandela waiting for Winnie,
I will wait
for the bliss in which my soul will bask

## Let Me Go

I loved you more than you hated yourself
In sadness, with care
No doubt you cared
but it's your heart you never shared
and I loved you so.

Don't say I never tried to wait
for our hearts to be wrapped in love,
but I guess it's time to leave.
after a grape-crush is fine wine,
And after pain is healing,
your heart will find its strut.

In the end, I lost you
Sure, it was in the cards.
But there's one good thing about you—
you broke my heart, no one ever could.

I hope you'll always know
We were good together,
we laughed, we cried, we kissed.
I don't know what letting go is meant to do
but packing my bags feels like a good place to start.

## Fool Or Sage?

I've figured to dance to the sins
of flesh and fantasy
as I fall into the muddy river of night stands.

I'm trapped like a cockroach
(My ancestors would've said: Uri bete rawira mumukaka)
—a trophy of night life.

Surprised?
............
this has been the history of all of us,
in the family Testament
going back generations.

J'ai changé
No lie,
Right down my eats : Less saccharine, and mozzarella sticks
less carbs and less cheese
less water & more whiskey
more—*(dhobhu)*: *Ndiri wenyu*
(I'm all yours)

There's no shame on me
For choosing to follow my own path
– fool or sage –
doesn't change whichever I chose to be

Blinded forever.
I'm dancing with the devil

who is wearing an angel's cloak.
Let me finish this journey somehow,
till we meet again…

## Hopes Will Bloom One Day

I found a wilting rose,
its blistered petals
crumpling down, and
I thought of you and how
one day I might wilt too…

I found myself promising the world
that I am wood
burning only for you.
Hopes will bloom one day,
as long as there is
a pinch of love in it.

Give me your hand,
let's wilt together
for the rest of our days.

## Once Upon a Midnight

Once upon midnight prosaic
while I pondered,
knocked by that ginger vin ordinaire,
its taste, tannin;
wondering in that haze of sleepiness
the silence was broken
as you knocked at my door.
I whispered an invitation and
your acceptance was ardent.

Your touch, your smile
beguiling my sad fancy into smiling
and your body smothered mine
as you covered every inch of me
with the heat of your tongue,
your mien with gentle hands and
soft fingertips welcomed promises
I could not decline.

## Your Favourite Song

With leaves and debris in our hair
glued on the bench under the tree,
our wild hearts and lies scripted lust
to ponder the sweet sky
in fantasy and fire,
obsession and desire.

The magnetic field drew us together
your hand behind my back
sending shivers down my spine into my legs
already shaky from the electric impulse,

forged in volcano of liquid soul fire
nothing could go wrong,
like beats of music
I breathed your heart's cadence
and synched my steps with your tempo

We tamed the soldiering rain
as I discovered a brilliance
in your almond eyes—
a hamlet of refugee stars

## We Were Guests

But while we drifted away today
we realised the road was taking us nowhere,
so, we won't be coming home.
Persons of all ages passed by: Some young,
                                         some old
the great globe reeled in the solar fire,
meanwhile the clear pebbles of rain
ceased to move across the landscapes,
over the prairies & deep trees,
the rivers & seas

We were guests at our own youth,
watching the world fly softly in the wool of heaven,
but never got the taste of kisses
out of our mouths
and danced naked,
grotesquely before mirrors

we were swinging on a continuum
between sublime & ridicule
love & capitalism had something in common—
pacing away to no relief
we thought we could earn it
and couldn't count on sheer luck;
in delusions
we fought upstream against the flow
wishing for what is not

# The Valleys Down

*-For the victims of Cyclone Idai*

In rolling hills
torrential rain and floods echo;
as tides of heat wave, and swift flurry of winds
pick up from the valleys of time.

Rivers and streams
rage with no mercy
gushing upon beings
to leave them no shelter.

From the east, wait on the winds,
catch the scent of salt
that wither our greener pastures,
livestock and fodder
roofs as rafts
all hurriedly handled to wrest from watery tombs.

We sway to and fro in a timeless search for
whatever can be saved,
worshipping mountains as they dissolve into dust
and peaks become bridges to other valleys
where twin atoms from the dust of time can meet

# Maputi neMabhodhoro

A vendor of proven love potions
never goes into emotions.
An organ grinding gypsy
who displays his moony teeth and joyous face

That feeble vendor who drops corn at our door
soothsayer on narrow by-pass, wayfarer
who uses a few pence he gets from shearer sweat,
to buy maputi and a wheelbarrow
then walks all the streets

Door by door calling out 'maputi nemabhodhoro'
a familiar echo
pushing the wheelbarrow till his back
can't carry no more, like the Son of man on Via Dolorosa

He is obliged to appreciate,
to live as an actor
    -    Stage change    -
But he's just a vendor
of cognitive provocations,
and academic totems
who sells the wheelbarrow
when maputi are exhausted.
And when the wheelbarrow is bought,
he sells the bottles
and walks home, his pockets heavy
with the days' coins for food and rent

## The Noise Maker

It was like broadcast waves
coming with news
of the roaring sea,
as they taught me 'empty barrels make the loudest noise'

Silence was a past legend
I knew nothing about isolation & silence
Still, they said I had no personality;
they loved silence & serenity
noise and chaos made them sick!

The habit of idle speech
became fortified in me
and I was mortified—
they'd soldered me into a cage,
with metals of their choice
but I refused to decay into their gilded life.

I never started that journey…
there was nothing to write for
but many of them have turned their backs on silence;
inventing devices that increase noise;
and distracting humanity from the essence of life;
– quiet contemplation, meditation –
In our quietest hour, the automatic ice-breaker
will duck and drop an ice cube
like a radio station that never sleeps.

## The Great MaShona Model

Drunk exhilarated men
shower her with tips
and go crazy when she drops down erotic thoughts
like ghosts wandering on the path
led by devils and demons,
breathing lamentation into their lungs,
they whisper and laugh
like a carnival of players
as her legs spin and swirl
down the pole like tongue on candy cane
before she whines…

I wonder how many times
have they gazed upon,
and undressed her in their minds,
run their fingers through her wavy chestnut hair,
lip-locked and engulfed her,
unzipped her fitted dress,
watched it drop from her body,
onto the ground to reveal her nakedness?

Eyes glow like embers in gloom
trying to overcome,
hers is a journey, coated by a cold black fear
that clutches her at night,
freezing their defeat

## The Night Passed

Nights passed by
snowfalls & solstices;
the moon shimmered with a cool perfume
as time passed in minutes and millennia
- the beach was scented with cold salt.
- the winds swirled with pride
- each rekindling, flickering lights of valour
as if life had engraved its story

The gleaming of random light,
and the torch bearer vanishing with an ox cart
on its way to Dorowa,
hearts dying like rotten logs lying on this earth –
a rooster singing at an unearthly height;
proclaiming the time is neither wrong nor right;
the heartbeat of fruit fall is heard in bed at night

The leftover mornings;
a slumbering starts
as the cruel dawn embraces the sun.

## Survivor

When this journey started long ago,
she was the captain of her own vessel
set adrift on an endless expedition to a destination uncharted.

Stepping on the ground
from the vessel that had moved her miles
into a land that was foreign,
she sagged, like a flag when wind drops,
questioning the depth of her existence

Anchored by chains in a dark community
that traded her like a commodity,
among strong-men
her ship was filled with many passengers,
of all ages and genders,
who boarded her deck without permission.

Gloriously free
from the encroaching wilderness
that caged her in anguish;
for every friend she lost
for every demeaning look
for every sleepless night
for every horrible fight
she was a warrior who struggled in battle
with a strong mind to ignore the prattle.

## We Shall Suffer If We Don't Hear

Endorsed in the dungeon of darkness,
conscious about the world, a trading market
where everyone cares about profits.
We know, we can't do a thing no more,
but be slaves of our wealth.

We shall suffer if we don't hear,
because we're doctors who die from their drugs;
We shall suffer if we don't hear
because the system they built will murder us;
We shall suffer if we don't hear;
because after a while
we'll conclude a life wasted in frustrating
sense of time dragging;
and become vagabonds
like Charlie Chaplin.

## Same Song

Songs we'd once say sweet things to
with words foiled in their coatings
Same, old songs on a new day
countless new songs walking in and out

The same corrupt government
Same old rules, same tortures
Same old Goliaths
Same old Pharaohs
Same old abuses
Same inequalities

Same victims
chucking the same chucking,
fighting the same fight.

## Rolling Stone

So tired of trying to talk to himself
into his own freedom
enslaved to ideas lingering in bones,
he couldn't get rid of these echoes,
the endless ravine
chasing a visage,
a vague voice whispering 'this isn't home.'

There was war inside
that he failed to keep locked tight
like mercury,
and entered the future as a shadow of the present self.

Farewell to comrades – in arms –
– in trenches – in dungeons – (the unknown) –
a song forever singing in his heart;
wherever he goes their pieces follow.

## Boats of No Captains

When the town comes to life
and light softens,
the ship sails away
while eyes follow the steady keel

the travellers with time to kill
and money to splurge disappear into the pitch-black cabins
as they become captives,
to gambling,
with drinks, food and entertainment so profuse.

the poor folk in a cold rubber boat
will soak to the bone
while mosquitoes draw their hungry song,
surveying the waterway
where they are employed.

the destination is the same,
songs of beauty and quiet
are sung by the waves,
mighty storms tell tales
that often batter the coast
while the voyager floats from war to war

## Pygmy Among Giants

My path is aimless, without an end
I don't dare mumble my mind,
I am a pygmy among the giants
my lords look upon treasures,
my ladies breathe fine perfumes
yet I resemble a peasant among the kings

I'm alone in a crowd
like a hermit with his gown

Will I ever find peace?
I do not know,
friends I may never meet taste like burnt rubber
and envy the sweet harmony that surrounds me,
but here they treat me as if
God is notably present in the country
while the devil takes the rest of the world to town
and I keep on waiting like a honeybee
in the mouth of a lotus, trying to fit in

## Blank Page

The words swim in my veins like backstrokes
waiting for my mouth to arrange letters
into messages with meaning;
like a soldier standing on the isle of choices,
picking between bazooka & grenade;
waiting for war

The ink jives its hips
into classic stories of sweet and bitter romance;
exhuming the past - into rhythm & flow,
to open sources of ethos;

This blank page is a canvas
that blends together & melts
into secrets of
                love
                        gratitude
                                  and
                                            redemption

# Buried Bridge

I stand on the bridge at midnight,
as the clocks strike the hours,
and the moon rises over the Victoria Falls
the two worlds connecting
like Olympic rings

From one bank to another,
Zambezi strides carry hope to sea,
beyond the floating bridge
where another world awaits;
there the master dances for the concubine.
The emperor falls
like a golden goblet sinking into the sea

Standing straight in the swirling straits,
the outdated bridge
whose chain bore great history and weight
looks like a submerging crown
jewelled with diamond raindrops
glistening in the tropical moon.

## The Devil Promised Evil at Full Throttle

The church bell rang in warning
before vows,
the devil laughed,
promising evil at full throttle
as long as our 'dream' would last.

Each step of lives—
a stairway to doom,
like tectonic plates our lives of pure chaos
reached havoc's shores.

We had a universe before the 'knot';
we had another planet in the house,
blissful destiny turned to horror,
smiles turned crooked & melted
into a catastrophe of warped teeth.

## Fight or Flee

The *tsapi*
*mataichengetera mabagwe*
This time cornless,
full of headless, skinless corpses;
survivors with frostbite smiles
consumed by madness, eating their dead

A group of them carrying chainsaws,
I could die upon those bloody blades;
I cursed the fall of the season,
backed out slowly,
hoping to avoid a dinner invite
or being part of the menu…

Distant sound of leather boots
echoed through the air,
their turn was coming – the waiting scared me more
than the biting hurt

Fight or flee
I was to decide;
sped like Usain Bolt,
they matched my speed

I was damned.

## First Slice of Bread

Drained from spite
wrapped in negative tags
stabbed with curses,
I felt like the first slice of bread in the bag
everyone touching me,
but not wanting me,

There was heaven, I thought
but echoes would abate after each storm
as if ancestors had tired of being ignored
      – Heaven's gate shut –

I couldn't bear the poverty
of being unwanted: I was a sacrificial lamb
        thrown to wolves like Daniel in the lion's den,
        by a society unwilling to see beyond colour, & DNA
I was Judas
to be blamed for society's wrong

## Addiction

A match in the biting breeze or in the snow
with each breath and blow,
each blink, every goal,
every foul & every score.

The touch of every tackle,
the goals scored & yellow cards
make me feel alive.

The speed of every dribble
with the ball glued on his feet,
like bubble gum,
nutmegs, throwing the opponents under the bus…
I'm happiest on the pitch,
where I make a date
with the love of my life.

## Awful Greed

I'm chaos & beauty entwined
hiding & bleeding
behind my mask;
thorns are my guard
—a delicate rose no one can take.

Like a sinister serpent with forked tongue
I dispatch hopes
drown dreams
plant self-doubt
and eat souls.

        This curse of destruct smudged me,
        a shell,
        a spectre lost in Black Sea,
        tossed away like Jonah on his way to Nineveh.

## Migration Was Better Than Home

The status quo had built a safety net
that excluded & punished their kin,
shunning the dreams engraved on their backs

It was a society spelled with brutal clarity
subdivision across; chained dreamers
already, they were walking zombies
that could consume but not digest

The suffering of women & children
raped & tortured under their father's watch
left scars of cruelty
deep & long-lasting as wounds of hell fire,
love & empathy were broken as
girls were exchanged in sex trade
& convinced to take drugs of all sorts;
the civil war had taken its toll
with no more morals or integrity,
men used human bones to pave their ways

All they wanted was to flee in hope of finding security;
but they didn't want to be the odd ones out
so they boarded boats…
water was safer than land

They crawled under border fences
because the other side was a better place to be

They chose to live in refugee camps

where they were guarded night and day
camp prison was safer than their home on fire

They spent days and nights in trucks
sometimes hours on foot;
no breaks, no smoking or lunch
because mileage travelled from this place
was far more precious than consumption of food

They deserved a better place,
their homes had become battlefields
and had them cast into desert & oceans
like beasts of no nation
that sang & died in the wilderness

Now we know why they walked,
migration was holy.
For Pharaohs had snatched all they had,
they risked their lives & left
for hope, need & escape.
They migrated,
because migration was better than home.

## Gukura...

The rondavel hut was inferno,
all we could do was flee
as we heard cries of women fill the air,
echoes of children crying for their parents,
every dream of innocence died
that night in Bhalagwe;
Somewhere the Führer
King Leopold II applauded
while even the devil wept in dismay.

Camouflaged— It was blood they needed like oxygen,
each bullet met flesh of citizens
cutting to the bone
flaying skins as if peeling grapes
until there was no heartbeat.

'Gukurahundi,' [1] the print said,
'The Brigade was the executioner
who killed for the State,
1000 miles away generals laughed.'

[1] The poem is dedicated to the Gukurahundi victims who were killed by the Zimbabwean state from 1983 -87

## If I Don't Make It Home

We just woke up to the sound of gunfire
Another war is at our doorstep and
I am writing this to you
smiling as I seize my weapons:

        'If I don't make it home, please
        Remember it wasn't because I didn't try;
        It was my job to keep you safe.
        I am the soldier who dived on a grenade
        so that comrades may live.
        Remember me by memories we shared—

        As we stand firm & fight, live a good life
        that we want you to live.
        If I fall on the battlefield, bury me
        when my country is safe.

Remember me for the human I was
Forgive me, for the wrongs I did
I am a soldier standing in the frontline
holding onto promises I made,
to be with you through a lifetime
If I don't make it home, remember me.'

## "I Must Arise!"

The sea of grief has no shores,
no bottom
the place I call home is no longer as tasty as it should be.
I have waited all my life,
dined on hopes,
drunk juices of torture,
because I was told to
I have waited for the sun to rise, to see a brighter future,
but my eyes were put out
by the boot of injustice,
choked by the yoke of servitude
forcing me to dwell in a spiral of silence
But I "must arise!"

## Letter from The Dead

I write to warn my friends
not to be shocked
when they come to the rendezvous
of the naked
where all travellers meet
and become Kings & Queens
of Solitude

Our hearts will once more sing
in a place of warmth & comfort
with souls like my own
in a place called Home

Having done with this earth
our mortal souls find no sorrow,
the mystery of our existence
is revealed in angel hugs & kisses
keeping the halo shining.

You can't get here by taxi,
wait like a pilgrim in exile,
for the Hour,
seeking hope from where murk peeps,
where everything ends, and begins
with the play of death & birth!

## Harare Hairarwe

Fragile sugars of time
fill a cracked hourglass
as I wander in the heart of Mbare,
boxed in what was once a golden suburb

I see rain drops falling down
the roof gutters
like tears falling down my cheeks,
parents tossing babies
hoping for the catch,
girls playing mariachi louder than the spectator
boys merrily running after the ball

Trains run on time
Passers-by rush for a seat
Garbagemen all in navy blue
and dazzling lime,
shovel till traffic swirls like storm debris,
the alley barbershop smells of old newspapers,
fetid diesel & paraffin
stale cigarette stubs fill the air

Across town
Sultan bastards dance in drunk repose,
greasing on champagne,
sugar delight – milk & honey
coated in jewels
as they bask in shadows
Of gold & coins.

Harare…Mbare
Beggars to billionaires
Vagrants & sophisticates
   – disgrace of the sleepless city –
      because Harare hairarwe

## Forced to Fuck Ghosts

The populace of Wadzanayi was fixed,
no one moved in or out,
time did not exist
there were neither children nor the aged;
two schools, two chapels
that no one set foot in,
business was perpetually closed
except the goldmine
& Tsamvi bar that opened after dawn,
customers entered but did not leave
unless their pockets were free,
the last customer always chancing upon Peggy
    —a girl once fluent in beds of bordello.

Habitués loved it when Peggy suggested going to her nest,
all eager,
silly fools,
thinking they were invited for a night stand,
they got trapped in a graveyard along Bushu Street,
forced to fuck ghosts
from grave to grave,
headstone to headstone
till the third cock crowed.

## Click-Clack

My history whirls around
the assemblage of wheels
of the scotch cart,
donkeys, cows
& futile load of burden,
pain, fear
CLICK CLACK

Unseen clocks,
Treacherous hoof shoes
Feasting on rocky roads
on carbon & dust from galloping
ravaging my innate skin
under the sheepskin blanket

Moments of comfort lasted
in these untamed mountains
wild in the craggy plains
where life lessons were learnt: Smoking gonan'ombe,
                                              milking,
                                                  hunting,
                                                gatherings

I was there once
like Jesus & the cross
yet my past lingers inside me
like treasured drift glass
tumbled smooth & tactile
a souvenir
I could never let go

## Affixed to the Slaughterhouse

It could be anywhere
they searched for black people's shadows
hunted them like terrorists,
walked on them like doormats,
burned them alive
centuries of years ago.

Affixed to the slaughterhouse,
smiling as bodies convulsed,
they enjoyed blood & guts
like witches on mass graves

Knives, hooks
Skulls & blood
A fer-de-lance
hiding in the Bible,
killing 'rivals' taking what was rightfully 'theirs'
yet the rival refused to die

# Cemetery

If you hate living
go to the cemetery: The dead lay beneath the earth,
                roots reaching out
                like tendrils wrapping them,
                In calm fellowship they sleep
                where graves are dark & deep
The living come today,
to read the marbles & go away
then come another day
when death comes to stay.

## Pain

One day they will shoot you too,
Oh pain!
from your flying wings;
your words, your instrument
your folk song will run out
you'll stay in your bosom.

You'd wreck the nervous navigator
and his ship of futile comfort,
you were as cheap as Woolworth beads

On the doors of our hearts
you've knocked oftentimes
ignored,
you stand in perseverance
on the doorsteps aching for our acceptation
in alluring rhythms, we retreat
but land on our breasts anyways

## Lost Diary

I feel lost in the diary
in which I've been writing for so long.
I'm afraid I have no idea at all
about certain key events!

The big ones that stick in my mind
remind me about colours of emotions;
solitude & desires
pain, suffering, joy
confusion, pleasure, brotherhood…

These memories make the writer,
it's getting harder for me
like bullets whizzing to spook me
and those that almost tore me into pieces

I know I lost you
but fragments of you
come back in flashes to paint this moment;
like my last sip of good drink

## How Two Cities Worship The Rising Sun

Lumining bright as fire,
the moon walks in glory
and looks on from above like Black Sea mountains,
clouds floating far through the azure sky…
shepherds & coffee tea drinkers of Trabzon
love mornings
because they know it will soon be night,
new days bring new possibilities

Within the Honde Valley
we wake up to fresh winds
and train whistles wondering
where it takes our cargo of dreams

Bewildered to the flirt in the tea plantations
the foggy clouds & polytunnels
two countries twin cities woo together
and can't blame the morning
for waking on the wrong side of the bed…
every dusk is a gift of life
that brings smiles on their faces

## Neighbour

He calls me 'Muchawa'
from a 'faraway country'
even though he knows I never set foot in Malawi,
his accusations towards me
fly like fishing rod lines
in the sea of words: Racketeer
                              toiling slut,
                                        mubvakure
        FUCKING LIAR
His kids are the mufana n'ina, figs of all seasons,
spite dominates their hearts
and unquench labour of thirst
they catch falling knives
like flies with closed mouths

they wipe the blood from their mousetraps
and burn it to warm themselves.
They have snake bones in their pillows...
...and throw parings in their soup

They are all pine & I'm apple orchard,
my apples never getting across
to eat the cones under their pine
but, one day they will leave behind
all the silver spoons
found in their mouths at birth.

## Like Two Odd Socks

I was the dream she never knew before:
She thought I was charmless
& uncouth
at least until that night when loneliness came
and I held her as none before

Pinned the wrong way round
her head between my arms
lips touching like moth to a flame,
hearts flying high on a gossamer wing
through a cloudless sky

Addicted to my violence
grinding against her like waves in a shore,
gasping & sweating
she matched my pace & indulged
in play till dusk

## Our World

The fire they put on us
lit our world

The fire we lit
consumed all that flooded
& aborted our passion

The more they pressed,
the lighter we became

as we waited for a spark to change our lives,
the fire hugged us like a mother's embrace
& left its epitaph in anonymous ashes

## Stash of The Street

I stashed you in poems
so that no one would know
how you lived on that street
or how you dealt with your strife

I kept everything in pre-history,
veiled when I laugh
but obvious when I cry

This heart stumbled into love
with someone's someone
and I knew it was pointless loving
what I couldn't prove was real

You eclipsed me like moon & sun dancing
and you were a thorn in my rose-filled life,
in love & waiting
to be touched by my hands,
but our moon & sun never danced

Sometimes I wonder what it would have been like
to stash you under my bed
like rocks beneath the sea,
till I spun back like a boomerang
to unpack you post-haste

It wasn't chaos
that dared us to change
but awareness of all failed comrades,

glimpses of tombstones carved
with names of compatriots calling our names

Back together after all these years
I see my childhood home,
a nostalgic voyage— my past decayed
and great glory where dreams arose.

## When the Time Comes

Oh man, you must die before you die
When the time comes,
The fuss of the world will ask: What are you going to eat,
                                      What do you want
                                      Where will you live?
You'll say, "I will eat death & wear shroud"
The grave will stay & stay there
"Will I take my grave, my money, my praise
my luxury & my friends?" you'll say.

Now or later, death will come
Your loved ones will become the past
but the past is your entrance key,
you'll see the seeds sprouting in the soil
and you will reap what you tilled

Relatives will cry,
bearing strength of Samson,
smashing every gravestone carved;
but you'll be winds that blow &
diamonds glinting on snow

you'll be sunlight on ripened grain
or the gentle autumn rain
that remembers nothing
as the blowing sand forgets the palm
where blue waters creep

# Glossary of Shona and Zimbabwean colloquial terminology

### FOOL OR SAGE?

**Uri bete rawira mumukaka:** you're a cockroach that has fallen into milk

**dhobhu:** slang for marijuana

**Ndiri wenyu:** I'm all yours

### MAPUTI NEMABHODHORO

**Maputi:** Zimbabwean corn snack similar to popcorn, usually sold by street vendors

**Mabhodhoro:** bottles, i.e., empty bottles usually sold by street vendors

**ne:** with/and

**'Maputi nemabhodhoro':** Corn snack and bottles

### THE GREAT MASHONA MODEL

**MaShona:** the Shona people collectively, particularly those of Zimbabwe

### THE NIGHT PASSED

**Dorowa:** a village in the province of Manicaland, Zimbabwe

### BURIED BRIDGE

**Zambezi:** fourth-longest river in Africa, the longest east-flowing river in Africa and the largest flowing into the Indian Ocean from Africa

### FIGHT OR FLEE

**tsapi:** (synonym of *hozi/dura*) traditionally tsapi/dura/hozi are mostly round small bins or huts made of mud and pole thatched with grass for the storing of grain harvest

**mataichengetera mabagwe:** where we kept corn

## GUKURA...

**Bhalagwe:** a remote, rural valley synonymous with the worst of post-independence violence in Matabeleland, Zimbabwe

**'Gukurahundi':** derives from a Shona-language term which translates to 'the early rain which washes away the chaff." A term used to refer to a genocide in Zimbabwe which arose in 1982 until the Unity Accord in 1987

## HARARE HAIRARWE

**Mbare:** a suburb in the south of Harare, Zimbabwe. First township in Harare, established in 1907

**Hairarwe:** never sleeps

## FORCED TO FUCK GHOSTS

**Wadzanayi:** a township found in the district of Shamva (Shamva is one of the seven districts in the Mashonaland Central province of Zimbabwe)

**Tsamvi bar:** famous bar in Wadzanayi, Shamva (Zimbabwe)

## CLICK-CLACK

**gonan'ombe:** a horn of a large beast used as a container or smoking pipe

## NEIGHBOUR

**'Muchawa':** originally used to refer Chewa people who came to Zimbabwe from Malawi but, misused to refer to Muslims since most early Zimbabwean Muslims came from the Chewa ethnic group

**Mubvakure:** someone who leaves one country to settle in another

**mufana n'ina:** female (human or animal) that is suckling, derived from a Shona idiom, *mbudzi kudya mufenje, hufana nyina/n'ina* (a goat feeds on cussonia paniculata tree just like its mother)

www.ingramcontent.com/pod-product-compliance
Lightning Source LLC
Chambersburg PA
CBHW012009090526
44590CB00026B/3934